eBay Subject Matter Expert

5 Weeks to Becoming an eBay Subject Matter Expert

Copyright © 2013 by Nick Vulich

FREAKING IDIOTS GUIDES

Table of Contents

Introduction

This book developed out of an eBay guide I wrote in 2007.

I targeted it towards new sellers and gave them a step-by-step process to help them become recognized as a subject matter expert in their chosen field of selling.

The advice I gave then will still work today for those sellers who take the time to implement it.

This book isn't going to be like other eBay books you've read. It isn't going to tell you anything about how to list items, how to price them, or even how to sell them. The advice I give you is going to do just two things:

1) Show you how to build positive feedback, and

2) Help you develop a series of eBay guides and reviews that will position you as a subject matter expert in the products you choose to sell.

I know what you're thinking - Wait a minute, Nick - I'm no expert. It doesn't matter. If you follow my plan you will soon be perceived as an expert.

Here's what becoming an expert can do for your eBay sales...

1) Your sales are going to skyrocket. People love to buy from an expert, and once they recognize you as one, they will keep coming back to buy more items from you. They will refer their friends who have similar interests.

2) Once people start buying from you, and get to know and trust you, price is no longer an issue. You will be able to charge higher prices than your competitors. Customers are going to keep coming back to you because of your product knowledge, and the breadth of your product line.

3) Other opportunities are going to open up for you if you watch for them. In my case, after fifteen years of selling on eBay and Amazon, I began writing about how to sell on eBay. Over the last year I've written six books about selling on eBay, Amazon, and Fiverr, and have sold thousands of copies of my books.

Most recently I have been featured in several magazine articles about how to sell on eBay.

Where will you go when your customers recognize you as an expert?

Only time will tell.

Why read this book?

Success on eBay seems easy enough. You list a few items for sale, wait for the money to roll in, rinse and repeat.

If only it were that simple.

The truth is: Anybody can put a few items up for sale on eBay, and score an occasional sale now and then. Being able to consistently sell items for a profit is not as easy.

What usually happens is new sellers decide to unclutter, and sell a bunch of unrelated items as they clean out the garage, basement, or attic. Some sellers break up a book collection or sports card collection and piece it out on eBay. The thing is once they finish selling the items they have they can easily find their sales have started to burn out.

They don't know where to turn next.

Other sellers can never seem to bring it all together. They have a great product line, they may even have the best price; but somehow, the sales don't seem to follow.

Let me share a little secret with you.

People love to buy from an expert. They want to know the person on the other end of the transaction knows what he's doing, and can answer whatever questions they may have. They want to know they can trust you.

In essence, potential customers want to know you're a subject matter expert in your product line.

Let me give you an example, I started selling on eBay fifteen years ago. My user name was Fifties Topps. That's all I sold. 1950's Topp's baseball cards. I sold a lot of them, in just about any condition you could think of. Some of them were like new; others were just plain ugly with pinholes, or chunks torn out of them. 1954 and 1955 were my favorite sets, and I specialized in them. Most days I would have a hundred or more auctions running at the same time.

Over time people noticed what I was doing. Many of them emailed me questions. What's the proper way to grade a card? What's the best way to store your cards? How did get started collecting?

You get the idea. Because I specialized in selling fifties baseball cards people saw me as their go to person for them. They told their friends about me. They bought cards from me. They asked me questions.

Eventually I started writing eBay guides. Many of them delved further into the questions customers were asking me. Before I knew it some of those guides received five hundred, a thousand, even twenty-five hundred page views.

The amazing thing about the whole process was in less than six months, I went from being an eBay newbie to an eBay expert in 1950's baseball cards.

Become an eBay expert

What I am going to outline here is a five step program. Not only will it put you on the road to becoming an eBay Top Rated Seller, but it will also make you an expert in your chosen field of sales.

The great thing is this plan will work for you whether you are new to eBay or an established seller. Keep in mind, trust isn't given – It's earned, and one of the easiest ways to earn trust is to freely give help to people who need it.

To make this happen we're going to use two eBay tools: Guides and reviews.

A **guide** is simply a tutorial on how to do something. It can be as simple as one sentence. "This was the greatest product ever; I lost ten pounds in under a week using it." Or, it can go on for thousands of words, and tell people everything they need to know about replacing the battery in a Kindle Fire HD, or it could be the recipe for a new chocolate covered bacon flavored cookie you personally developed. The possibilities are endless, as eBay will let you write a guide on just about any topic under the sun.

A **review** is your opinion of a book, movie, or product you have used. Once again, the sky is the limit. eBay will let you write a review about anything you want.

The really great thing is: Every time someone reads your guide eBay gives them a minimum of two ways to find your products. At the top of each guide they display a header with your user id, the number of feedbacks you have, and a link to your store. Under that they show three products related to the guide. If you're really lucky, sometimes they will feature one or more of your products there; it just depends on how close of a match they are.

Many times eBay will also display three items for sale from the author's store below the guide. Buyers can scroll through a list of items generated by eBay, or they can click into any of your items that tickle their fancy.

Either way, it's a win for you because it offers several more ways for buyers to find your listings. And the cool thing is, when they find you this way, they already know you from your guide, and understand you are an expert in what you are selling. As a result, they're going to be more likely to do business with you.

It's like the story of the car salesman who rushes out to greet you the moment you hit the new car lot. The minute he asks, "How can I help you?" or "What are you folks looking for today?" – Your defense shields immediately go up, and you blurt out "just looking," and start to move away. It's a natural reaction. Everybody does it.

But, if that same salesman starts out by saying, "That's a nice looking Camaro you're driving. I bet you had some really great times in it." You're likely to share a story about the time you were speeding down that old country road and …

You get the idea. Your guide warms your customer up, and lets them know you're a real person who's concerned about them, and willing to help.

It's you're opening line, or you're ice breaker. It gets your customers attention.

Author's Items for Sale See all of this seller's items

1859 South American Earthquakes Arica Peru Equador	1888 Roosevelt Remington Ranch Life in Far West	1895 Frances Willard Women's Christian Temeprance Union
$25.99	**$19.99**	**$19.99**
Buy It Now	Buy It Now	Buy It Now

One other thing to keep in mind with eBay guides and reviews is they are indexed by Google, so any one searching for the topic of your guide has a good chance of finding you when doing an internet search.

Writing your first guide

Writing a guide can seem like a formidable task, especially if it is the first one you've ever attempted. But, it really doesn't have to be that hard.

If you're planning on something short, the easiest way to get started is to approach it like you're talking to a friend. Tell them what it is you have to say; include all of the necessary details; and tell a few stories about what happened when you or someone you know used this approach. That's really all there is to it.

If you're considering a longer guide, you might want to write a short outline first. An outline will help you organize what you want to say, and it will also help you to keep on track, and make sure you've included all of the necessary details.

For example, if I was going to write a guide about how to ship your item internationally for new sellers, my outline might look something like this:

. Introduction

. Why listen to me / my qualifications

. How to tweak auction to add international selling

. How to pick a shipping method / carrier

. Where to get help

. What to tell buyers / set delivery expectations

. Legal disclaimers

. Final words of encouragement

My outline is short, to the point, and will help keep me on track when writing my guide. Your outline should also be flexible enough to let you add or subtract ideas once you get started working on it.

You can see the finished guide in a later section of this book.

_____

The main thing to remember when writing your first few guides is to not stress out over grammar, spelling, sentence structure, etc., etc.

Your first and main concern should be to offer high quality, actionable information readers can use to enhance their knowledge, or perform a new task, such as learning how corner damage affects grading of 1950's baseball cards. Readers will overlook a lot, if you can give them useful information they can take action on.

Another thing that keeps people from writing guides is they're not sure what to write about.

Oftentimes people think all of the best topics have already been written about. Other times they just can't think of anything to write about.

The truth is you just need to get in the habit of writing. People are desperate for knowledge on just about any subject out there. If you write it, someone is going to find it and read it.

Let's go back to the example of someone selling baseball cards. Obvious guide topics are new releases, card grading services, star players, trades, football – baseball – basketball in season. "How about those Bears?" You can talk about your favorite team, or maybe a favorite series. Did you see a major league game as a kid that got you started collecting? Talk it up. Maybe you went to school with a kid who's a star player for the Cubs or White Sox. Tell people what he was like back then.

What do you collect? Who is your favorite player? Maybe you could pick two or three players a week and do short guides detailing their careers, or some of the special cards they've been featured on.

The available topics are endless.

I should also mention there are some things you shouldn't write a guide about. One of them is new products you just put up for sale. A lot of new sellers do this, and it really doesn't make much sense. They will tell you, "Hey, we just got in a 'lot' of new Pokémon Games," or "I just listed a retro yellow polka dot bikini."

These really aren't guide topics. A better way to do it would be to write a review of Pokémon White or Pokémon Silver, or you could put together a guide discussing the various Pokémon games; when they were released; and the differences in them. This information would help to set you apart as a gaming expert; especially if games are one of the main products you carry.

Hopefully that helps you see the difference. A review gives your personal opinion about, or your experience using a particular product; a guide shares information about a particular subject. A guide helps people to learn more about something.

Saying, "Hey! I just got in a bunch of so and so," makes you look like a spammer. It doesn't help anyone.

It's really just a matter of getting started. The more information you put out there, the more people are going to read your guides, and find your items on eBay.

I know sometimes it seems like you're taking a stab in the dark, and it seems like a longshot anyone will notice what you're doing. But I guarantee you, if you keep putting guides out there, people are going to find your listings, and they're going to buy from you, and tell their friends about you.

It's happened to me hundreds of times. It can and will happen to you, as well.

Product reviews

If you want to sell more products, take time to write thoughtful reviews about your experiences with different books, movies, and products.

Everyone, no matter whether they are spending one dollar or a thousand dollars, hesitates about whether to click the buy button or not. It's human nature.

A good review eliminates some of this tension and can make you more willing to give that new product a try. Look at Amazon. They built a business out of letting everyday people post reviews of books, products, and movies. They know people want to be assured they are making the right decision. And, they want that reassurance to come from other people who are just like themselves, not from some guy who makes his living writing reviews.

That's why the eBay platform for writing reviews is so important for growing your eBay business, but only if you approach it the right way.

Reviews should be more folksy and personal than a guide. You want to inject a lot of your personality into them, especially when you are reviewing movies and books. This is your chance to connect with your customers and let them know what you're all about. If they like what you say and they enjoy your selection they will be back for more of your words of wisdom.

The key takeaway here is to be sure and inject as much of your personality as you can into each review. Make it fun to read. Be honest. If you didn't like the movie or book tell people, but also tell them why you didn't like it. For example: "Overall it was a great movie, but I just didn't like the way it ended. There was no closure." "I was lost through the whole thing. I couldn't figure out why…"

If you're reviewing more serious works, like books on history or science, you should keep a more professional tone. Talk about the premise of the book, how the author presented his topic, and if you feel qualified – tell readers what you think. Does the book make sense; does the conclusion match the evidence the author presented; if not, what do you think should have been done differently.

Don't be afraid to tell people where the author went wrong. Academics do this all of the time. They use reviews to add another piece to the puzzle and to get their two cents worth in. A great book I would recommend on this topic is **They Say / I Say** by Gerald Staff and Cathy Birkenstein.

The same thing goes if you're reviewing a product. Take a few minutes to introduce people to it and what it does. If the product is surrounded by a lot of hype, tell people why you bought it, and what your expectations were. Next tell them what actually happened. What experience did you have using the product? Was it good, bad, or mixed? Share your feelings about the product, and finally, make a recommendation. Should readers buy it or pass on it.

Keep in mind – The whole idea is to encourage people to purchase from you, so you want to keep your reviews on a more positive note. When I'm on the borderline, I like to throw this out there at the end of my reviews. "That's my opinion. Read it yourself and let me know what you think."

Think about it, every eBay store out there is going to have the new movie release from Tom Hanks or Sandra Bullock, and you can only go so low on the price to get people to check your item out. But if you write a review and let people know what you thought about the movie, including the good, the bad, and the ugly of it – They just might click into your store or on the movie if it's offered for sale in your store.

I've included some sample reviews I've written at the end of this book to give you some ideas of what might work for you. Keep in mind you want to develop your own style and tone. Over time it will come naturally. One of the reasons people will keep returning to your reviews is because of you. If they trust you, and like what you say, they're going to keep returning to your reviews to get your take on that new movie or book.

Don't let them down.

Week 1 - Set Up Your eBay Seller Account

This week is all about preparation.

If you're new to eBay the first thing you need to do is set up your seller account. Be sure to pick out a name that describes your business - Vintage Sports Cards, Sports Memorabilia Stop, or Fifties Topps. My current eBay ID is history-bytes. It's short; memorable because of the play on words; and gives people an idea of what I am all about. Whatever you choose, make the name memorable and easy to remember.

If you already know what product line you're going to sell, great. If not choose two or three categories that interest you.

Search your category to determine who your competition is. Get out your handy dandy notebook, and start writing. What are the competition's eBay seller ID's? What kind of product are they selling? How many pictures do they include in each listing, and what quality are they? How many angles do they shoot pictures from? Is their product graded, or are they selling filler cards? How many feedbacks do they have, and are they quality feedback? Read through their feedback comments to get clues as to why customers are buying from these guys. How much are they charging for shipping? Do they ship first class, priority mail, or by some other service?

This week is all about deciding what type of product you are going to sell, and getting a feel for what's out there. A lot of people go into eBay half baked, thinking they can sell whatever comes along, but by doing this they limit their ability to make real money long term. To be successful on eBay, you need to select a niche (your own tiny segment) and run with it.

Every product you add to your mix should relate to your niche, and compliment the other products you sell.

For that same reason you need to study your competition. You need to know who they are; how long they've been on eBay; their pricing strategy; what they charge for shipping; and what their feedback says about them.

If you don't know what your competition is doing you can't distinguish yourself from them, and neither can your customers.

The other key thing you need to work on if you're new to eBay is developing positive feedback. Good feedback tells potential customers that you can play well with others. The easiest way to get feedback starting out is to make a number of small purchases.

Buy five or ten small items from sellers in your niche to start building your feedback. Record how long it takes to receive your items? Check out the packaging when your purchases arrive. How well are they packaged? How much did actual shipping cost compared to what they charged you? Was the packaging adequate?

More importantly, did the product meet your expectations? Did it match the description the seller gave in the item listing? If not, what was different? How did that make you feel when you opened the package and discovered it wasn't quite what you expected?

Finally ask yourself the question every eBay buyer is going to ask themselves after each purchase, "Based on this experience, would I buy from this seller again?"

Week 2 - Start becoming an expert

No selling this week.

Go back to week one, and look at those categories you chose to specialize in. This week you are going to write five eBay Guides. It's time to dazzle the eBay world with your intelligence. Write about particular cards - Like variations in Mickey Mantle Rookie Cards - Buying vintage wax packs – How to put together a Fifties Topps set - or Bargain shopping at Sports Card Shows.

This week is all about making you an expert in your field. The writing doesn't have to be top quality, or anything fancy. It just needs to be informative. The more tips you can share on collecting, storing, or grading old cards - the more people will perceive you as an expert.

Buy five more items from your competitors to keep building your feedback.

Week 3 - Share Your Knowledge

No selling this week.

Continue writing guides. Your goal this week is to add at least five more guides to your collection. If you need ideas look at the cards you are going to sell. You can focus on individual cards or players. Talk about the sets, and any variations in them. There are thousands of people who want to read this info. If you're at a loss for topics, write about your Hank Aaron or Ernie Banks Cards. Talk about grading cards, and put pictures of various cards in there showing the different conditions.

Remember you are proving to the eBay world you know your topic inside out, and you should be their go to guy for what you sell. Anyone can sell a baseball card. You are freely sharing your knowledge and expertise with everyone.

Buy five more cards to build your feedback, and continue checking out your competition.

Week 4 - Preparing to Sell

No selling this week. But we're getting real close, I promise.

This week you're going to write five more guides, and buy five more cards to continue building your feedback.

You also want to start scanning or taking pictures of the first batch of cards you are going to list. By now you should know the kind, and quality of pictures you want to include. Get them all ready. Another thing you want to do is to start crafting your auction descriptions. What standard information are you going to include in all of your auctions. Put together your selling and return policies. What are you going to say about individual cards? How much are you going to charge for shipping?

What you're trying to do is develop a template you can use over and over again in each of your listings.

Most of your listings will probably contain the same basic information. If you're selling baseball cards you need to include the year, manufacturer, card number, condition, catalog value. Include an area for more detailed information. Some sellers like to go into great detail and write a short bio for each player featured on the card they are selling. Others stick to basic information and condition. How much information you choose to include is totally up to you. After this you will want to mention shipping, return policies, and any other information you feel is important.

Your final template could look something like this:

Year:
Maker:
Card Number:
Condition / Grade:
Catalog Value:
Description:

All items are shipped by first class / USPS, and include tracking and insurance where appropriate.

Here at Fifties Topps we understand that buying on line can be a little scary at times. That's why every item comes with a 100 % Satisfaction Guarantee. If you are unhappy for any reason we will gladly offer a full refund.

That's a very simple template, but it gives all of the information your customer needs to make an informed decision. You can always add more to it as time goes on and you make more sales.

A lot of sellers use custom templates with lots of images. Templates give your listing a unique and interesting look, but as eBay has evolved fancy templates can limit your visibility and sales. Right now mobile (shopping on cell phones and tablets) accounts for nearly one third of online shopping. Very soon it will account for half or more of all online purchases.

And here's a dirty little secret you need to know – When mobile shoppers search for items, eBay will not display your listing if it uses a template or has embedded pictures in it. That means you are eliminating from one third to one half of your potential customers by trying to fancy things up.

Think real hard before using any HTML templates. Is looking good worth losing customers? It's a decision you have to make for yourself.

Week 5 - Start Selling

This is the week you have been waiting for.

It's time to start listing your auctions. You should have at least twenty to twenty-five feedbacks by now. And, if you have written all of your guides you should be a top 5,000 or 10,000 reviewer. You are a responsible member of the eBay community and should be perceived as an expert in your field ... and, you haven't made a single sale yet.

Think how good it will be once you get the ball rolling with a steady stream of sales.

How much better does it get?

Sample Guides

Here are four guides I originally published on eBay over the past ten years.

I've tried to include some examples of different topics, and a short explanation of why I wrote each particular guide. Hopefully reading these guides will give you an idea of how to structure your content.

Also keep in mind, eBay does allow you to add illustrations to your guides. If you are writing about grading baseball cards you can include illustrations to represent the different grades. Doing so will make it easier for people to take action on what you're writing about.

Tips on Buying Old Magazines and Books

(*As history-bytes on eBay I've purchased thousands of old books and magazines, and this is a guide I wrote to help readers over some of the speed bumps they might encounter when they purchase old books and magazines.*)

As a collector of old magazines - I've learned there are a few things you need to be aware of before purchasing.

1.   A lot of the old bound magazines being sold today have been stripped of the most valuable prints. This is especially true with Scribner's and Century Magazines from 1890 to 1920. A lot of the Parrish, Wyeth and Christy prints among others are being removed before the magazine is listed. When this happens the dealer can sell the prints separate from the bound volume. Normally, this is not a problem, unless you are using a collector index, and over bid because you think those prints are included.

2.   Condition is often mis-stated. Bad condition is often covered up with words like "good condition for its age." The fact is - Just because a book is 100 or 150 years old, does not make it bad. Condition should be stated in terms of the binding. Is it tight, loose, or pulling apart? Are the covers attached or at least present? Are there loose pages? Are all of the illustrations called for present?

3.   Another thing you need to look for is foxing and spotting. Is it heavy, moderate, or very light. Be sure to look at pictures to ensure your judgment meshes with the seller's description.

Pictures tell a thousand words. Be sure to look at the pictures included. If defects are mentioned in the description - does the seller have pictures to illustrate the problem. If you are just looking for a reading copy this is not all that important, but if you are putting together a collection - Pin the seller down. Ask for pictures of any problem areas, and agree in advance on return privileges if the item is not as you expected.

I have purchased thousands of bound magazines and books on eBay, and the one thing I can tell you is - That one of a kind item will come around again next week, or next month - so if you are not sure on the item...Let someone else bid on it. Keep your eyes peeled for the next copy.

Why Would Anyone Purchase An Old Magazine Article?

(I wrote this guide to help explain my business to potential customers. I sell old articles excerpted from magazines, and a lot of people no matter how many times you state it in the item description don't understand that they are getting pages from an old magazine or book, not the entire book. This guide let me explain that, as well as give people ideas why they may want to purchase my magazine articles.

I actually use this guide as the main introduction to my business. It is prominently displayed in the sidebar of my eBay store. I think it is so important to my eBay success that I had Fiverr celebrity puppet, Professor Hans von Puppet make a three minute video reading it. The video is hosted on You Tube, and embedded at the bottom of every eBay listing I run.)

It's a question I get every day, and not just from customers. Friends and family think I've lost my marbles when they see my twenty thousand plus old magazine article collection, and if you just look at the space it takes up - They may be right.

But the truth is old magazine articles offer a unique view point on historic events. Over the past seven years I have sold nearly twenty thousand magazine articles here on eBay. Many have gone to museums, historians, scientific researchers, libraries, and even to some really neat collections - like: The White House Historical Society,

The Royal Museum in Jamaica, the Fort George Historical Society through a presentation from the local boy scouts, the Fort Sill Museum, and to various castles in Europe (for articles and illustrations dealing with them).

Here are just some of the reasons you may want to consider collecting historical magazine articles -

• Often times they are the only source of information on a particular subject or person.

• Unique perspective. Especially during the Civil War, many articles were reported and written as they were taking place. As a result, the info may not be 100% accurate, but they give a great flavor for what was happening at the time.

• Awesome pictures. Harper's Monthly, Scribner's, Harper's Weekly all offer awesome woodcut illustrations of events and characters. Unless you know where to look for them, most people would never find them. Around the turn of the century Munsey's Magazine was one of the great periodicals offering 100's of illustrations of kings, queens, soldiers, presidents, expositions, and other events of the day.

• Family history. A lot of times we are able to hook people up with articles written directly about their famous and not so famous relatives. Other times the articles fill in information on how distant relatives lived, or the events they participated in - battles, coal mining, religious movements. You name it, and someone in the past wrote about it.

- Teaching Aids. It's one thing to talk about Johnny Appleseed to your third grade class. How about if you enhance the experience by reading an 1870's Harper's article on Johnny written during his lifetime, illustrated with woodcuts of the man.

- Historical Research. Any event you can think of was written about in many of the graphic magazines from the 1800's. They offer a great sampling of perspectives for researchers, writers, and publishers. The pictures also bring life to many drab historical characters.

- Fun. It's interesting reading. Fact filled. And fun.

- Great Gifts. Do you have a fan of the old west. What could be more interesting than an 1867 article filled with illustrations of Wild Bill Hickcok. Is your husband, or son a civil war re-enactor or enthusiast - How about an 1865 article full of illustrations on Sherman's March to the Sea, and the Burning of Atlanta. Are Indians your thing - 1863 saw a great article covering the Indian Uprising in Minnesota. If you lean more to the Spanish American War, there are hundreds of articles out there covering every battle and player involved.

Trust me. No one can read just one. Once you start your collection, you are going to wonder why it took so long to get started.

Early History of Harper's New Monthly Magazine

(One of the best sources for early magazine articles and illustrations is Harper's New Monthly Magazine. They chronicled just about everything happening during the time period, and were illustrated with hundreds of unique woodcut illustrations. Because so many of the articles I sold were taken from Harper's, I decided to offer my buyers a short history of the magazine.)

Harper's New Monthly Magazine debuted in June of 1850. It started out republishing a lot of English Literature, but over time evolved into one of America's greatest general interest magazines.

Some of the early articles covered: an eleven part series by Benson J Lossing on the War of 1812, an 1865 reminiscence of Abraham Lincoln written just after the assassination, John Smith & Pocahontas, Boquet's Expedition, Stephen Douglas writing on the Dividing Line Between State and Federal Politics. Any topic you can think of - there was probably something written that touched on it. During the Civil War Harper's profiled the Civil War Generals - Grant, Sherman, Sheridan, Rosseau, and Fighting Joe Hooker. Other Civil War articles covered Sherman's March to the Sea, Railroad Adventure and Big Shanty, Philip Kearny and the Change of Base, Civil War in Texas & in the Wilds of Arkansas. Still another series of articles detailed Personal Recollections of the Civil War.

One of the great early illustrators was Porte Crayon - He had an 1850's article on the Baltimore and Ohio Railroad. He illustrated the Personal Recollections of the Civil War Series, and later in the 1870's did an illustrated series on the Mountains.

1857 saw an early portrait of Santa Claus illustrating Clement Moore's 'Twas the Night Before Christmas. The 1870's saw an article entitled the Spirit of Christmas Past, with lots of fanciful Christmas illustrations.

Other memorable articles from the 1850's include - Kit Carson, Thomas Jefferson & Monticello, Mountain Man James Beckwourth, two articles on Gold & Silver Mining in Nicaragua, Adventures in Madras, Adventures Among Samoan Cannibals, Ibis Hunting in Louisiana, Sugar Production in Louisiana, George Washington at Morristown, An illustrated history of Mount Vernon.

The period from 1850 to 1900 was some of the magazines greatest for articles and illustrations. Most of the illustrations were wood cuts, and closer to the Spanish American War in the late 1890's the use of pictures increased. Frederic Remington was a featured illustrator in the 1880's and 1890's - with many cavalry, Indian, and cowboy illustrations.

In literature, Harper's New Monthly published Charles Dickens' *Bleak House* and *Little Dorrit*, William Makepeace Thackery published *The Virginians* and *The Newcombes, Romola* by George Eliot was also published in Harper's.

Another great thing about Harper's New Monthly is that it was collected in bound volumes by all major libraries and numerous collectors, thus the abundance of copies available today on eBay. Any given week collectors can pick up just about any volume of Harper's for anywhere between $10 and $25 each.

International Shipping for the Rest of Us

(After I was on eBay a while I started writing guides to help new sellers get started selling on eBay, as well as offering information that could help more experienced sellers expand their tool kit. This is one of the more popular guides I wrote in this category.)

International sales can seem a little scary at first. But they are really no more challenging than making a sale in the United States, and they can open up a new world of selling possibilities for you.

I've been selling on eBay for roughly seven years now, and my international sales have grown from 1 or 2 per month, to nearly 25% of my sales. And, the good thing is - Of the 2500 items I've shipped internationally; only two have not made it to their recipient. That's a record I would love to have for my domestic sales.

If you really want to take on the international market you need to tweak your auctions a little, and decide in the sell your item form which areas you want to ship to. I've heard horror stories about shipping to Russia, Poland, and Mexico - but, I've never once had a problem with any shipments to those countries. Anyway, eBay gives you the option to select which areas, or countries you are willing to ship to. If you're the cautious type, maybe pick Canada and the UK. If you're bolder, and have a "go for it attitude" - select worldwide and see how it opens up your sales possibilities.

The next step is deciding on your shipping method. I do all of my shipping through the post office, because they're close by, easy to deal with, and relatively inexpensive. UPS, FED EX, and DHL also offer many great shipping options depending on what you are selling.

My suggestion would be to stop in or call the carriers you are thinking of, and find out exactly what is involved in shipping your items.

With the post office I can tell you - The customs form is the main difference. You need to declare the value of every item you are sending, because many countries charge a duty, or tax on the item. One suggestion I would make is to have all of your customs forms filled out and ready to go before you head for the post office. This makes it quicker for everyone, postal staff and other customers.

You will also be faced with a number of shipping options - but it really comes down to ground (sort of like taking the slow boat to China - 4 to 10 week), and air (7 to 14 days). If you can, always pick the faster method. No one likes waiting, and if you take the slow boat option, you're going to be getting a lot of emails and phone calls from your international customers wondering where their item is.

I would also suggest putting plenty of information in your auction listings detailing your international shipping methods, expected delivery times, and preferred payment methods. The more information you give up front, the less problems you are going to have after the sale. It's all about managing expectations - Most eBay buyers want to pay when they are ready, and receive their item yesterday. Your job is to politely explain all the details, while not discouraging purchases, or sounding too harsh, with all sorts of obnoxious rules.

One final thing you are going to hear all of the time is: Can you say it is a gift, or not declare the full value? Don't do it!!! If you are caught, it is a felony.

Give international shipping a chance, and watch your sales skyrocket.

More Sample Guides

I am also including several sample guides I've written just for this book to give you a better idea of what you can do. Please take a few minutes to read them over.

International Selling Made Easy

Many new and experienced eBay sellers shy away from international selling, oftentimes because they're not sure what to expect. Some of them are afraid to attempt filling out the customs forms, and others have heard horror stories about missing packages, or sellers who demand refunds saying they never received their items.

These are all valid fears and I'm sure there are some delivery problems and bad eggs out there. With that said, international selling is still one of the surest ways to increase your eBay sales.

I've been selling internationally for the past fourteen years and I can tell you from experience – International shipping most often goes smoother than domestic shipping. In that time I've mailed over 4,000 packages to every area of the globe and only two ever went missing. I've had a number of packages take six to twelve weeks to get to their destinations, and a few have been returned as undeliverable (the round trip took 67 days). But overall, that's not bad. I've had packages going just a few hundred miles away take three to five weeks to deliver or that have just mysteriously disappeared in transit.

The biggest problem with international shipping is tracking; or the lack of tracking options. If any problems arise in shipping eBay requires tracking and proof of delivery, or they will issue a refund to your buyer. If the value of your shipment is over $200 they require a tracking number plus signature delivery. Even with the most expensive shipping options tracking is nearly impossible for international shipments, and for that reason, a lot of people have shied away from it.

About a year ago eBay launched a new international shipping program that made shipping to foreign destinations a snap.

What they did was to essentially make shipping internationally no different than shipping domestically.

eBay contracted with a courier service in the United States. After your customer pays for their purchase, eBay sends you the address of a designated shipping center in the United States. When they receive your package the shipping service readdresses it; fills out all of the proper customs forms; collects duties; and forwards it on to your customer.

Once the package is received at the shipping center you're no longer responsible for it.

How much easier can it be?

That's the basics of the **eBay International Shipping Program**. You can select it in your auctions as the first choice under international shipping.

With that said, let me talk a little bit about why you might want to not use the program.

1. It's expensive for your customers. eBay shows them a shipping price that includes postage, forwarding fees, and duties. For example, my standard international shipping fee is $7.00. eBay charges $31.00 to $33.00 for the same service. Customers are going to experience a bit of sticker shock when they see that fee.

2. Every time you add a middleman to something, there's an extra chance something might go wrong. It's another chance for your item to get lost or damaged in transit.

I use a combination of shipping services. Some of my listings use eBay's International Shipping Program. Others have standard shipping where I post the item internationally myself.

Shipping internationally is really just a matter of filling out the proper custom forms. I would suggest you have the folks at the post office or UPS help you out with the first one or two, after that you will be able to do it easily enough.

I actually use Stamps.com for all of my mailing. The software automatically imports the address. All I need to do is input the weight and declare a value for the package; it automatically fills out the customs form and spits out a label for me.

Whichever service you decide to use, remember shipping internationally is really no different than shipping in the United States. It also opens up a whole new market that will give your sales a quick boost.

History of Munsey's Magazine

Munsey's Magazine debuted as a weekly in 1889. Not long after that it switched to a monthly format, and by 1893 they were selling nearly half a million copies per month. In 1929 it merged with Argosy Magazine, and soon after that into All-Story Magazine. You can find links to the individual volumes on line by visiting Wikipedia.

Some of the early articles covered: The Spanish American War; a series on prominent American families that covered the Washington's, Lee's, Harrison's, Polk's, Dana's, and more; coverage of the Galveston hurricane; the Hatfield-McCoy Feud; profiles of American presidents, statesmen and educators; and lots of historical reporting.

And did I mention the illustrations? Munsey's offered some of the finest illustrations of its time. In its time hundreds of movie and theatre actresses graced its pages; Theodore Roosevelt was pictured numerous times; European Royalty popped up on many of the pages, as did the society women intent on marrying into the royal families.

Munsey also featured a great selection of artwork: William-Adolphe Bouguereau and Edouard Bisson were two of the most prominent. Just about every month saw articles on current artists including George Grey Barnard, James E. Kelly, Giovanni Boldini, C. D. Gibson, and more.

They also published a Junior Munsey Magazine, lavishly illustrated for young adults. What I like best about it was they didn't dumb it down. It was the same size as the regular version and featured similar stories rewritten for younger readers. The illustrations were all the same high quality as in the regular version.

Collectors can find bound volumes of Munsey's on eBay selling for from $10.00 to $25.00. Keep in mind the magazine was in decline in the 1920's, and after 1922 most issues contained no illustrations.

1955 Topps Baseball Set

It's no secret the 1955 Topps Baseball set is my favorite.

They're slightly larger than current day cards, measuring 2 5/8 inches tall times 3 ¾ inches wide. The color was fantastic, and they have an all-around awesome look to them. The front features a head shot of each player, next to a shot of them in action. They also sport a snazzy team logo at the top of each card. The reverse side gives a detailed player bio and stats.

The set features many of the all-time greats of the game: Hank Aaron, Willie Mays, Sandy Koufax, Ted Williams, Duke Snider, and Yogi Berra. Notable rookies that year were Sandy Koufax, Roberto Clemente, and Harmon Killebrew. The only big name player missing was Mickey Mantle; he was under an exclusive contract with Bowman. Topps solved that problem the next year by buying out the Bowman line.

The set consisted of 206 cards, and as anyone who has tried to build a collection knows, the high numbered cards from 161 to 210 are the hardest to locate. The rarer cards in the set are of Willie Mays, Yogi Berra, Duke Snider, and Harry Agganis (who died suddenly in June of 1955).

If you collect this set there are a few problem areas to watch out for. The cards are subject to doctoring.

Unscrupulous dealers have been over-fond of erasing the colored background around the borders to make the centering better than it actually was. The card backs also present problems because of the images on the back it is often hard to detect creases. People have been known to rub a spoon over the creases in an effort to eliminate them. These cheats are easily uncovered during grading when the cards are examined under a bright light.

For my money, the 1955 and 1954 Topps Baseball sets are two of the most desirable sets on the market.

Check them out for yourself and let me know what you think.

Sample Reviews

(I wrote the following product reviews to give you an idea how easy it is to position yourself as an expert. Most of them took less than a half hour to research and write.)

Topps Finest Baseball 2013

Topps Finest baseball cards mark their twentieth year with the 2013 set. I still remember when the first set was released in 1993. They were an immediate hit at all the card shows that year. Prices were high and everyone gambled on a pack or two hoping to pull that shiny Refractor card.

So it's no surprise Topps is harking back to those early days to celebrate their twentieth anniversary. They have a retro design to honor that set.

The basic hundred card set features a combination of veteran players and rookies. There is also a great selection of parallel cards for those addicted to the chase. Eight basic Refractor sets are available with an extremely limited number of each card.

1) Printing Plates. (1 available)
2) Super Refractors. (1 available)
3) Atomic Refractor. (5 available)

4) Red Refractor. (25 available)

5) Gold Refractor. (50 available)

6) Orange Refractor (99 available)

7) Green Refractor. (125 available)

8) X-Fractor. (149 available)

Hobby boxes are packed with two mini-boxes containing six packs each. Every master box promises an **Autographed Rookie Refractor** and an **Autographed Jumbo Relic Rookie**. The **Autographed Rookie Refractors** have the same design as the base set. The player photo is set against a dotted background highlighted by the team colors.

Topps Finest 2013 also features a number of insert sets. Highlights include: **Triple Autographs** which are numbered to five; the **Rookie Redemption Program** which gets card holders a not yet announced autograph card numbered to 100; a **1993 Finest Refractor** set numbered to 25; and **Finest Maser Refractors** numbered to 25. Several other limited inserts are also available to add to the excitement.

Cards are packaged 12 packs to a box, five cards to a pack, and boxes are currently selling on eBay in the $85.00 to $100.00 range.

Is $.99 the New Free? The Truth about Launching and Pricing Your Kindle Books

By Steve Scott

Steve Scott is one of my favorite Kindle book authors. He seems to be a straight shooter. His books are normally dead on, with no BS, and no filler.

This one is no exception.

As a Kindle book author I can tell you a lot of things have changed on the platform over the past year. It used to be all you had to do was offer a free book and thousands of people would grab a copy. When your free days were over your book would get an immediate boost, and you would normally receive a nice surge in sales.

Today it's a whole different ballgame. People have more choices, and they're not as likely to pick up a free book. I've had days where my book has hit the top three hundred in the Amazon Free Store giving away just 500 copies. After the giveaway, it's a struggle to sell five copies the first week.

That's the way it is.

Scott acknowledges "free" isn't a sure thing anymore, especially for established authors. His observation, thus the title of the book, is 99 cents is becoming the new free. That was sure true the first few weeks after this book was released. I observed dozens of authors dropping their books to 99 cents in hopes of getting that sales burst.

Does it work?

I've tried it in the past with several of my books, and I think it depends on the category your book is published in. My history books respond more to a free giveaway; my ecommerce books do better with a 99 cent promotion.

I've never tried a 99 cent launch before without doing free giveaway first.

Will 99 cents work for you? Maybe, maybe not. The only way you're going to find out is to give it a try for yourself.

My final take-away, if you're a writer – you really need to read Steve Scott's books. They will help you build your toolkit so you can sell more books.

Check this one out for yourself, and let me know what you think.

Hogan's Heroes: The Komplete Series, Kommandant's Kollection

Wow! Talk about bringing back memories. We waited for this show every week when I was a kid. The fact is I still remember how to count to five in German from listening to Sergeant Schultz count off the prisoners at roll call.

When I was in college you had to time you supper break just right at Burge Hall in Iowa City, because Hogan's Heroes ended at 4:30 and again at 5:00, and that started the big rush towards the lunch room. Sadly you had to miss the last few minutes of one of those episodes unless you wanted to wait forever to eat.

The cast of characters was outstanding:

Bob Crane played Colonel Hogan.

Werner Klemperer was the slightly off kilter Commandant, Colonel Klink.

Sergeant Schultz was played by John Banner.

Robert Clary was the love sick Frenchman, Corporal Le Beau.

Larry Hovis, played Sergeant Carter, the kid with a thing for explosives.

And, who could forget Richard Dawson, as Newkirk the conniving Englishman.

Of course there were many other regular characters, Major Hochstetter, of the Gestapo; General Burkhalter, and his sister, Frau Burkhalter, who seemed to have a thing for Colonel Klink; Marya, the Soviet spy who always seemed to make her way back to visit the gang at Stalag 13; and of course, there was Fraulein Helga, Colonel Klink's sexy secretary, played by Sigrid Valdis (she assumed the role after the first season).

This box set contains 28 DVD's containing all 168 episodes. My thought grab a couple Big Gulps filled with Diet Coke, a couple bags of Corn Curls, some peanut M & M's and get ready for nearly eighty hours of great fun.

At roughly sixty dollars for the entire set, it's about the price of taking a family of four to the movies, if you throw in popcorn and drinks. Not a bad deal.

Final Thoughts

For starters, I want to thank-you for hanging in there and making it to the finish line.

If you're serious about growing your sales on eBay, this book will help you on your journey. Everywhere you turn people are desperate for advice. There's so much information available, people are drowning in it, and they want – no, they need you to tell them what to do.

Think about it, ever since we were kids at school we've been programmed to respect authority. Listen to teacher. Do what the babysitter says. Listen to your boss.

That's why being perceived as an authority is so important to your success on eBay. People listen to Doctor Phil; they respect Barbara Walters; back in the early days of television news Uncle Walter (Cronkite) was one of the most respected and trusted authorities out there.

If you follow the advice laid out in this guide, people will look at you the same way. But, you have to do it the right way if you want to be successful.

If you take a look at my guides they are professional and straight forward. They explain how to do something, for example, how to use the eBay international shipping program. They give you more information. The guide detailing the 1955 Topps Baseball set introduces you to it; highlights the main cards in the set; and tells you some of the difficulties involved in collecting it. The guide about Munsey's Magazine gives you a brief history of the magazine; tells what type of content and illustrations you can expect to find in it; and ends by letting you know what current selling prices are on eBay.

Each guide also expresses my views. I use the international shipping program for some of my listings, but I also ship some items on my own. It's no secret that the 1955 Topps Baseball set is my favorite. I like what they did with Munsey Junior.

Be sure you do the same thing with each and every one of your guides. Give people the facts, but also give them little glimpses of yourself; it will help you come off as more genuine and helpful.

This is even more important when you're writing your reviews. Ninety-nine percent of the people out there writing reviews are going to say the same thing. Jurassic Park was about dinosaurs. Paul McCartney was one of the Beatles. This book was about "blah blah, blah blah."

Put yourself into it, and people will remember you and think "ah-ha, this guy is the real deal."

You can see that in my guide about the Hogan's Heroes boxed set of DVD's. How many other people have memories of racing out of their dorm room seconds before the show is over to beat the lunch line at the University of Iowa? In my review of the 2013 Topps set I shared all of the information most anyone needs to know about that set. I also revisited my days of doing baseball card shows in the early nineties. This detail lets readers know I'm not some flash in the pan collector who just jumped into selling baseball cards for a quick buck; I have a twenty year history in this game.

And, if you read my review of Steve Scott's book, you discovered he's my favorite author writing about Kindle books. You also found out I'm not some "want to be" when it comes to Kindle book marketing and publishing. I've been out there in the trenches with Steve Scott trying to figure the game out.

Every guide and review you write should do the same thing. They should divulge a little more about you; letting readers know you have a stake in the game; you're out there in the trenches every day doing the things you're talking to them about. You need to let them know you really are the expert.

Play hard to get. Let your story work its way out gradually. Share little tidbits about yourself in each guide and review you publish. It's sort of like dating, you want to show your moves, but you don't want to give it all away on the first date. Save some of the good stuff for your next encounter. It's the kind of magic that will keep readers coming back for more.

Continue writing your guides and reviews, mention them in your listings, and let people come to you gradually. They will respect you even more for taking the soft sell approach.

You don't have to tell them you're the expert; they will discover that for themselves, and they will let you know with dollars and cents.

Breaking news from eBay

eBay announced several new tools today (10/22/2013) that can help you transform your business.

The first one that affects this guide is the new eBay Seller Profile. Every time someone clicks on your seller ID it brings them to the new Profile page.

Here's what you see at the top of the Profile page.

Upload your picture. Above that you can upload a profile picture similar to what you would do on Facebook. I put my blog header there for now. I will have to have it redesigned for a better fit. The recommended size is 1200 x 270 pixels (maximum image size 4 mb).

Below this they show five items from your store, and a scrolling link to view more images.

Below that is a link to another new feature - eBay collections. Sorry I haven't had a chance to play with this one yet, but I will try to explain a little bit about it here.

According to eBay, collections are a whole new way to showcase your products. They offer an image gallery to explore a limited selection in more detail. I would liken it to eBay's version of Pinterest. They recommend you put no more than ten to fifteen images in each collection, and have at a minimum five to ten collections for people to look through.

The main takeaway, eBay is trying to make shopping a more visual experience.

Profiles also make Reviews and Guides more relevant, because as you scroll further down the Profile page your top three product reviews and guides are prominently displayed. It would be a shame to let all of that prime selling space sit idle.

Take advantage of this new opportunity to grow your eBay business.